anythink

21st Century Junior Library

Oviraptor

by Jennifer Zeiger

CHERRY LAKE PUBLISHING * ANN ARBOR, MICHIGAN

Published in the United States of America by Cherry Lake Publishing
Ann Arbor, Michigan
www.cherrylakepublishing.com

Content Adviser: Gregory M. Erickson, PhD, Dinosaur Paleontologist, Department of Biological
Science, Florida State University, Tallahassee, Florida

Reading Adviser: Marla Conn, ReadAbility, Inc.

Photo Credits: Cover and pages 10 and 14, ©National Geographic Image Collection/Alamy;
page 4, ©Lourens Smak/Alamy; page 6, ©iStockphoto.com/Syldavia; page 8, ©Universal Images
Group Limited/Alamy; pages 12, 16, and 18, ©Stocktrek Images, Inc./Alamy; page 20, ©Xavier
Fores - Joana Roncero/Alamy.

LIBRARY OF CONGRESS CATALOGING-IN-PUBLICATION DATA
Zeiger, Jennifer.
  Oviraptor/by Jennifer Zeiger.
    p. cm.—(21st century junior library. Dinosaurs and prehistoric animals)
  Summary: "Learn about the appearance, habits, and history of the Oviraptor"—Provided by publisher.
  Audience: K to grade 3.
  Includes bibliographical references and index.
  ISBN 978-1-62431-162-8 (lib. bdg.)—ISBN 978-1-62431-228-1 (e-book)—
ISBN 978-1-62431-294-6 (pbk.)
  1. Oviraptor—Juvenile literature. 2. Dinosaurs—Juvenile literature. I. Title.
  QE862.S3Z454 2014
  567.912—dc23   2013004928

Cherry Lake Publishing would like to acknowledge the work of
The Partnership for 21st Century Skills.
Please visit www.p21.org for more information.

Printed in the United States of America
Corporate Graphics Inc.
July 2013
CLFA13

CONTENTS

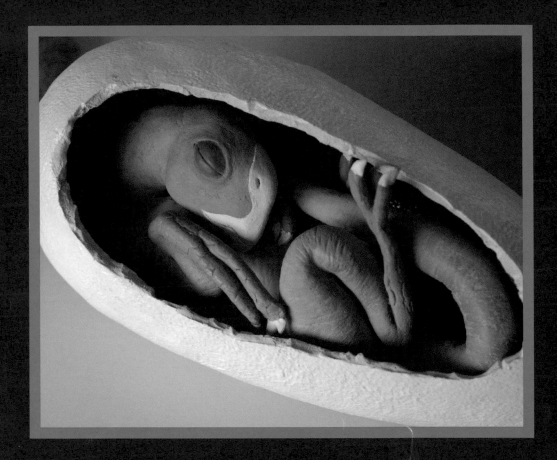

This model shows what a baby *Oviraptor* may have looked like while still growing inside its egg.

What Was *Oviraptor?*

It is a hot, sunny day in the desert. A beaked dinosaur sits on top of a nest of eggs. Everything is quiet. Suddenly, the wind picks up. A wall of sand blows quickly toward the dinosaur. The mother dinosaur huddles over its eggs. Soon the dinosaur and its nest are buried.

Scientists have found *Oviraptor* with eggs or near nests.

This dinosaur is called *Oviraptor*. It lived about 75 million years ago. Its home was in a region now called Mongolia. Like all dinosaurs, *Oviraptor* is now **extinct**.

Ask Questions! What was Earth like 75 million years ago? What plants and animals were around? Were they different from those you see today? Was the weather warmer? Colder? What other questions can you think of? Ask a parent, teacher, or librarian for help finding answers.

Scientists are not sure how
Oviraptor was colored.

What Did *Oviraptor* Look Like?

Oviraptor walked on two legs. These legs were long and strong for running. The dinosaur's two arms were shorter and thin. Its hands could twist at the wrist. Three clawed fingers on each hand could grab and hold **prey**. *Oviraptor*'s long tail kept it **balanced** as it ran.

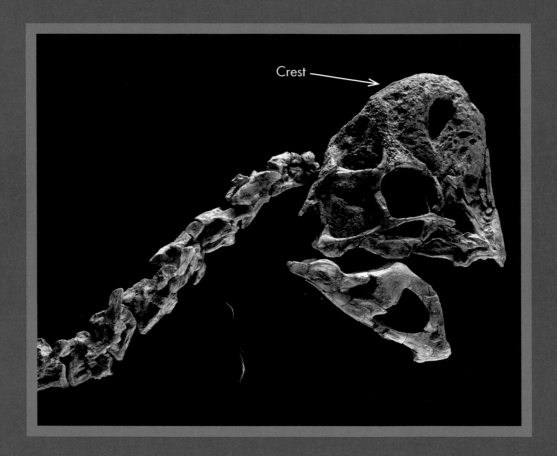

Crest

Oviraptor's crest was made of bone. It looked like this, as part of the skull, or head.

The dinosaur's head was oddly shaped. On top was a large, curved **crest**. Two large eyes were on either side of its head. *Oviraptor* did not have a mouth full of teeth. Instead, its mouth was a beak. The beak was sharp, pointed, and strong. It looked a lot like a parrot's beak. This dinosaur had a nasty bite!

Oviraptor might have had feathers,
much like modern birds.

Oviraptor was about as long as an adult human is tall. But the dinosaur was not heavy. It weighed around 60 pounds (27 kilograms). This is about the same weight as a golden retriever. Like a bird, *Oviraptor* had lightweight bones. This meant it could run fast without using much energy.

Look!

Scientists often compare dinosaurs to birds. Many scientists argue that dinosaurs are closely related to birds. Look at a picture of *Oviraptor*. How does the dinosaur look similar to a bird? How does it look different?

Oviraptor parents probably caught small animals to feed their young.

How Did *Oviraptor* Live?

Oviraptor was a **carnivore**. This means that it ate meat. Experts think it ate mostly small animals, such as lizards. Lots of small **mammals** lived in the same area as *Oviraptor*. These probably made tasty snacks for *Oviraptor*, too.

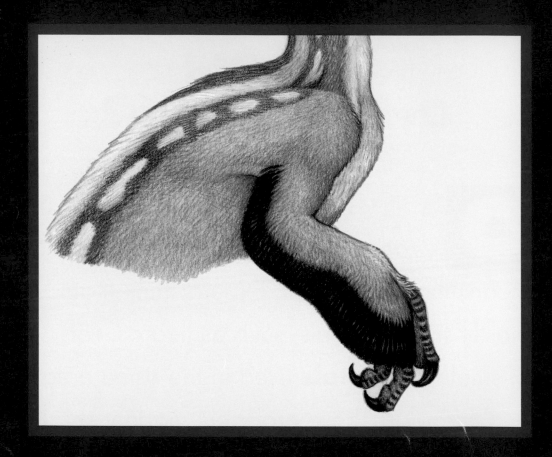

Oviraptor's large, sharp claws helped it catch and hold prey.

Oviraptor used its good eyesight to spot prey. It quickly chased its prey down. The dinosaur probably caught and killed its prey with its claws. Then the dinosaur could take a bite with its sharp, powerful jaws.

Scientists have found whole nests of
Oviraptor eggs.

Dinosaurs laid eggs. *Oviraptor* cared for its eggs before they hatched. It might have sat on top of the eggs. This would keep them warm when the weather was cold. *Oviraptor* may have had feathers on its arms. These would shade the eggs from the hot sun.

Visitors can see *Oviraptor* fossils at
museums around the world.

Scientists know about dinosaurs by looking at **fossils**. Adult *Oviraptor* fossils have been found with dinosaur eggs. At first, experts thought *Oviraptor* was stealing the eggs when it died. But scientists studying the fossils found this was incorrect. The eggs were *Oviraptor* eggs. The adult *Oviraptor* was protecting its own eggs!

Think!

Oviraptor means "egg thief." But the dinosaur did not really steal eggs. What do you think a better name would be?

GLOSSARY

balanced (BAL-unst) steady, able to stand without falling

carnivore (KAHR-nuh-vor) an animal that eats meat

crest (KREST) a showy growth on the head of an animal

extinct (ik-STINGKT) describing a type of plant or animal that has completely died out

fossils (FAH-suhlz) the preserved remains of living things from thousands or millions of years ago

mammals (MAM-uhlz) animals that have hair or fur and usually give birth to live babies

prey (PRAY) an animal that is hunted by other animals for food

FIND OUT MORE

BOOKS

Gray, Susan Heinrichs. *Oviraptor*. Mankato, MN: Child's World, 2010.

Hughes, Catherine D. *First Big Book of Dinosaurs*. Washington, D.C.: National Geographic, 2011.

WEB SITES

Animal Planet—*Oviraptor*
http://animals.howstuffworks.com /dinosaurs/oviraptor.htm
Read tons of interesting facts about *Oviraptor*.

Natural History Museum— Examine *Oviraptor*
www.nhm.ac.uk/kids-only /dinosaurs/who-was-oviraptor
Learn what scientists know about *Oviraptor* and what they're still trying to figure out. Examine the evidence, and decide for yourself!

INDEX

ABOUT THE AUTHOR

Jennifer Zeiger lives in Chicago, Illinois. She writes and edits children's books on all sorts of topics.